x976.4 Georg.C

George, Charles, 1949-

Texas /

Seeds of a Nation

Texas

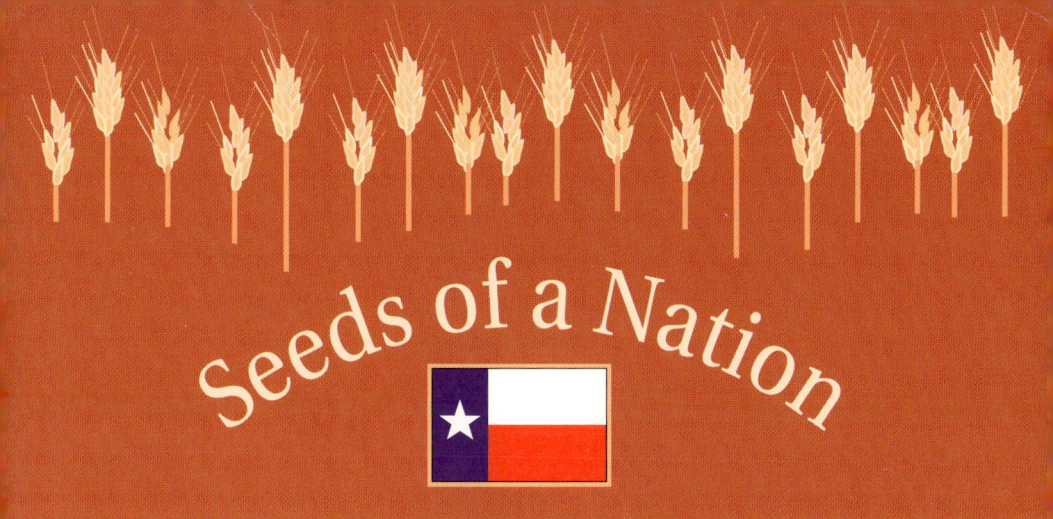

Charles George and Linda George

EVANSTON PUBLIC LIBRARY
CHILDREN'S DEPARTMENT
1703 ORRINGTON AVENUE
EVANSTON, ILLINOIS 60201

KidHaven Press

KidHaven Press, an imprint of Gale Group, Inc.
10911 Technology Place, San Diego, CA 92127

Library of Congress Cataloging-in-Publication Data

George, Linda, 1949–
　Texas / by Linda George and Charles George.
　　p. cm. — (Seeds of a Nation)
Includes bibliographical references and index.
　Summary: Discusses the earliest inhabitants of Texas, the arrival of European explorers, the establishment of Spanish missions, the arrival of Anglo-American settlers, the Texas revolution, and statehood.
　ISBN 0-7377-0648-1 (alk. paper)
　1. Texas—Juvenile literature. 2. Texas—History—Juvenile literature. [1. Texas—History—To 1846.] I. George, Charles, 1949– II. Title. III. Series
　F386.3.G46　2002
　976.4—dc21

2001000062

Copyright 2002 by KidHaven Press, an imprint of Gale Group, Inc.
10911 Technology Place, San Diego, CA 92127

No part of this book may be reproduced or used in any other form or by any other means, electrical, mechanical, or otherwise, including, but not limited to photocopy, recording, or any information storage and retrieval system, without prior written permission from the publisher.

Printed in the U.S.A.

Contents

Chapter One 　　The First Texans	4
Chapter Two 　　Explorers, Missions, and Comanches	12
Chapter Three 　　Rising Conflict	19
Chapter Four 　　War, Republic, and Statehood	27
Facts About Texas	39
Glossary	41
For Further Exploration	42
Index	44
Picture Credits	47
About the Authors	48

Chapter One

The First Texans

Texas is a leading manufacturing and agricultural state in the south-central region of the United States. The term *texas* (or *tejas*) is the word Native Americans in the area used to describe themselves to Spanish explorers. It meant "friends" or "allies," and today, the state motto of Texas is "Friendship."

Covering more than 267,000 square miles, Texas is bordered on the east by Arkansas, Louisiana, and the Gulf of Mexico; on the north by Oklahoma; on the west by New Mexico; and on the south by Mexico. In the United States, Texas ranks as the second-largest state in land area and in population, with more than 20 million people.

The first people to live in what is now Texas may have arrived ten thousand to thirteen thousand years ago. They were **nomads,** moving from place to place in search of food, water, and shelter. Those who settled in east Texas developed cultures much different from those in west Texas. One

The First Texans

reason for this was a difference in climate. East Texas receives plenty of rain, has lots of rivers and streams, and is home to abundant wildlife. West Texas is much drier, its rivers are smaller and farther apart, and wildlife is scarce.

By the time the first Europeans came to Texas in the early 1500s, three native cultures lived there. The Caddo, a well-organized farming society, lived in east Texas. People of the Plains Indian culture—Tonkawa and Lipan Apache—lived in central and northwestern Texas. Much later, in the 1700s, three other Plains tribes entered the state: Comanche and Kiowa in west Texas and Wichita in the north, near the Red River. Karankawa and Coahuiltecans lived along the Gulf Coast and in south

TEXAS'S PLACE IN THE UNITED STATES TODAY

Texas

Texas. They had the least developed cultures in Texas, very similar to their prehistoric ancestors.

Caddo

The Caddo became the most advanced Indian culture in Texas. The tribe lived in an area where food and water were easy to find. They lived in villages of beehive-shaped homes built of wood, reeds, and grass. These structures were forty to fifty feet tall (about as tall as a three-story building) with an opening in the ceiling to let out smoke from the central fire pit. Their homes were sixty feet wide (a little wider than a standard basketball court), large enough for three or four families.

Native American Tribes of Texas

- Present-day Cities
- Present-day State Border
- Present-day Border with Mexico

The First Texans

The men of the Caddo tribe painted their faces and wore feathers in their hair.

Caddo men painted their faces and bodies, and wore feathers in their hair. They usually went naked in the summer or wore a **breechclout**—a leather thong worn around the waist. In winter, buffalo-skin blankets kept them warm. Women wore deerskin skirts and blouses and braided their long hair, tying it with red-dyed string made from rabbit hair. Everyone wore deerskin moccasins.

The Caddo hunted small and large game, including bears and buffalo. This provided meat, clothing and blankets, and bone tools. They planted **maize**—a type of corn—as well as beans, watermelons, squashes, pumpkins, sunflowers, and tobacco. Women dug roots to mix with nuts or fruit or to grind into flour called **pinole** to make bread. This bread was used for trade.

Each tribe had a chief, and tribes came together to form a **confederation**, or alliance. The Caddo Confederation had one chief above all the tribal chiefs, much as each state in the United States has a governor, and the nation has a president. The confederation had existed for over thirty-five hundred years before European explorers came.

Texas

Early Caddo people built huge earthen mounds that looked like flat-topped pyramids. These mounds served for burials and ceremonies. Some of their mounds can be seen today in northeastern Texas and in Louisiana. They worshiped Earth Mother, Corn Goddess, the Sun, Sacred Fire, and their main god, **Ahahayo**, or "Father Above." They believed Ahahayo created everything, rewarded good behavior, and punished evildoers. The Caddo kept "Sacred Fire" burning day and night, believing their culture would exist as long as the flame burned.

Tonkawa

West of the Caddo, near present-day Austin, lived the Tonkawa. Instead of living in permanent villages, the Tonkawa were nomads. Because they were always moving, they used various kinds of shelter. Sometimes they lived in small pit houses that were covered with brush. At other times they used tepees made from poles and animal hides or **wickiups**, which were crude round shelters made from branches and covered with grass.

Like most Plains Indians, the Tonkawa depended heavily on the buffalo. Unlike other Plains Indian groups, however, they also ate fish, crawfish, clams, and mussels from the Colorado and Guadalupe Rivers. They also ate roots, herbs, seeds, and nuts. They especially liked pecans. The only meat they would not eat was wolf, and this was for religious reasons.

They believed they were descended from a mythical wolf. *Tonkawa* means "People of the Wolf." They also never farmed. They considered themselves to be like

The First Texans

Nomadic tribes of Texas never lived in permanent shelters.

wolves, and wolves do not farm. The Tonkawa buried their dead, and they sometimes practiced cannibalism, which they believed gave them the strength and courage of their enemies.

Karankawa

Like the Tonkawa, the Karankawa were **hunter-gatherers**. Their nomadic lifestyle was simple, but they were more warlike than the Caddo or the Tonkawa. Traveling along

Texas

coastal areas in bands of thirty to forty people, they often broke into smaller groups to search for food.

They lived in portable wigwams, called *ba-acks*, large enough to house seven or eight people. These homes were circular frames of willow poles covered with animal skins.

They were strong and healthy. Men stood up to six feet tall, were quite muscular, and had long, sloping foreheads. They believed a flattened head was a sign of dignity. Women tied their infants' foreheads against flat rocks. By leaving children bound for extended periods, their skulls flattened.

Partly because of their size, the shape of their heads, and the way they decorated their bodies, Karankawa warriors looked fierce. They cut small slits in their noses, chins, and chests and inserted bones or pieces of cane, much like people pierce their ears and wear earrings today. They also tattooed their faces using blue dye. Besides their fierce look, they also had a strong odor. To keep away swarms of mosquitoes and biting flies, they smeared themselves with shark oil and alligator grease.

Karankawa warriors inserted bones into their noses and tattooed their faces.

The First Texans

They ate a variety of foods. From the sea they caught oysters, porpoises, mussels, alligators, and turtles. They also hunted wild game, such as deer, bears, and javelinas (wild pigs). To supplement their diet, they gathered acorns, nuts, and roots. They did not plant crops.

The Karankawa also used cannibalism in their religion. They tied a captured enemy warrior to a post. Then, one by one, they sliced off a piece of the live victim's flesh. They roasted the flesh and ate it while the victim watched in horror. They believed they were consuming their enemy's bravery, courage, and magical powers along with his flesh.

Native American groups in Texas coexisted for centuries. They traded with each other and lived, for the most part, in peace. In the early 1500s, though, another group arrived, bringing with them a totally different culture. Clashes between these new arrivals—European explorers and settlers—and the native peoples of Texas were inevitable.

Chapter Two

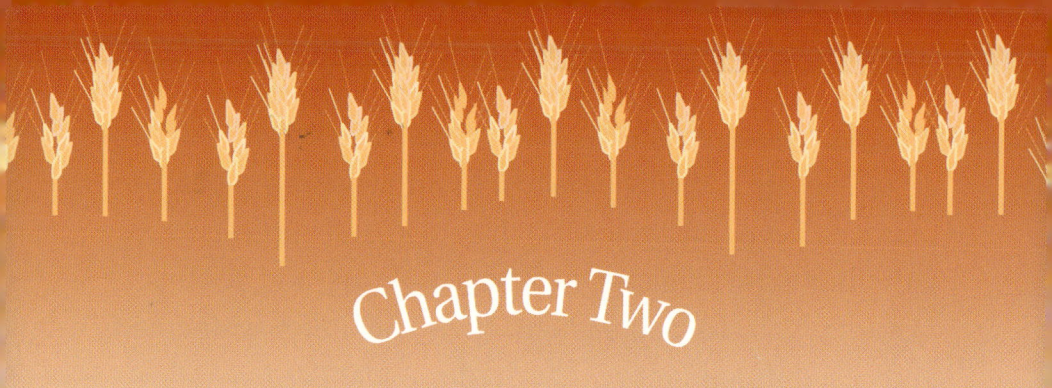

Explorers, Missions, and Comanches

The story of Texas centers on relations between people of different cultures. Before Europeans arrived, relations existed between widely different Indian cultures across the state. Once the Spanish and French arrived, the story shifted to relations between Europeans and Indians. To most Europeans, Texas Indians seemed violent and primitive. Native Americans must have been equally bewildered by and suspicious of these visitors.

For early explorers and priests, the relationship ranged from well-meaning attempts to educate and Christianize the Indians to deliberate attempts to destroy them. What started out as a cautious friendship with Europeans eventually led to the destruction of Native Americans' way of life.

Native Americans and Europeans had very different ways of life.

When Spanish explorers first came to the New World, they sought two things: riches and a route to Asia. They found great wealth in the Aztec Empire of Mexico, and they assumed there must be more wealth in other parts of the continent. Their search led them to the Gulf Coast of Texas.

The first reported contact between Spaniards and native Texans came in 1528, when members of a shipwrecked expedition washed up on Galveston Island, near present-day Houston.

Cabeza de Vaca

Álvar Núñez Cabeza de Vaca was one of the leaders of that expedition. He wrote about his experiences, giving the Spanish their first eyewitness account of Texas.

Texas

Cabeza de Vaca explored Texas after staying with the Karankawa for several years.

Cabeza de Vaca had been part of an expedition sent to explore Florida and the Gulf Coast. When a hurricane capsized their boats, survivors made their way to land on November 6, 1528, naked and starving. They named the island Malhado, meaning "Island of Doom."

The Karankawa found Cabeza de Vaca and the other castaways, brought them food, and gave them shelter. The Spaniards lived with them for several years, slowly gaining their trust. Finally, Cabeza de Vaca and three companions headed west, hoping to find some of their countrymen in Mexico or California, where earlier Spanish exploration had taken place. In 1536 they finally made their way to a Spanish settlement on the Pacific coast of Mexico.

Explorers, Missions, and Comanches

Other Spanish Exploration

Cabeza de Vaca wrote about his eight-year experience—his life among the Indians, his travels, and fantastic stories of wealth. His report led Spanish authorities to send other explorers to Texas.

In 1540 Franciso Vásquez de Coronado led an expedition north from Mexico. Searching in 1541 for the fabled Seven Cities of Gold, his men briefly explored part of today's Texas Panhandle. They failed to locate any riches, but by crossing the territory they strengthened Spain's claim.

One year later another Spanish expedition explored east and central Texas. Spain sent Hernando de Soto in search of riches in what is now the southeastern United States, but he also failed to find any great wealth.

Because of the failure of both Coronado and de Soto to locate treasure in Texas, Spanish authorities lost interest in the region for over a hundred years. Few explorers

Coronado searched for the Seven Cities of Gold in what is now part of Texas.

were sent, and only a few small settlements in west Texas were built. Not until the 1680s, when explorers from France showed interest in the region, did Spain again move into Texas.

Spain Fears a French Invasion and Begins the Mission Era

In 1684 René-Robert Cavelier, Sieur de La Salle, the first French explorer in Texas, landed on the Gulf Coast near Matagorda Bay with nearly two hundred French colonists. They built Fort Saint Louis and explored inland. After three difficult years, La Salle was killed. Disease and Indian attacks killed most of the other colonists, and the fort was burned to the ground.

When Spanish officials in Mexico City heard of the fort, they feared France was staking its claim on the territory. Not knowing about the fort's destruction, Spain sent Captain Alonso de León to capture the French and remove them from Texas. His expedition on April 22, 1689 found only abandoned ruins. The next year de León went back to east Texas, along with priests and soldiers, to prevent further French settlement.

One member of that expedition, Father Damián Massanet, built the first mission in east Texas in 1690—San Francisco de los Tejas, near present-day Nacogdoches. Between 1690 and 1721, Spanish priests built five missions in east Texas. Priests attempted to convert the Caddo to Christianity and make them loyal subjects of Spain. Floods, disease, and Caddo resistance, however, caused many missions to close.

Explorers, Missions, and Comanches

Several missions were built in east Texas including Mission Concepción.

Beginning in 1718 Spanish priests built missions in the San Antonio area. The first of these was San Antonio de Valero—the Alamo. These missions were successful because natives in the San Antonio area were more willing to accept the Spanish way of life. They also needed protection from another group of newcomers—the Comanche.

Horsemen of the Plains

The Comanche moved from their homelands in the Rocky Mountains into Oklahoma and Texas in the early 1700s. Excellent horsemen, they soon became lords of the plains. They eventually swept southward, controlling much of eastern New Mexico and western Texas.

Texas

open democracy, and the early Mexican government was not very stable.

When Mexico became independent in 1821, it had an emperor. Three years later it became a republic, with a democratic constitution. Between 1824 and 1834, Mexico changed from a democracy to a dictatorship, back to a democracy, and again to a dictatorship. This worried most Texans, both Anglo-American and *Tejano* (Texans of Mexican descent). Differences between Mexican officials and Anglo-American settlers in Texas eventually led to conflict.

Early Immigrants

Early in the nineteenth century, before Mexican independence, Anglo pioneers filtered into east Texas from the United States, settling on small pieces of land without

American pioneers usually had to pass through rough terrain to reach the West.

Rising Conflict

permission from the Spanish government. Farmers were attracted to east Texas by cheap, fertile land and plenty of rainfall. Because east Texas was relatively isolated, the Spanish government, which owned the land, said little.

Large bands of American Indians also came to Texas, forced from their homelands in the United States. Cherokee from the southeastern United States moved into the area north of Nacogdoches. Alabama and Coushatta tribes settled in present-day Sabine County. Groups of Shawnee, Delaware, and Kickapoo came to the region seeking land from the Spanish and later from the Mexicans.

Through the 1820s Mexican officials openly encouraged American settlers to move to Texas. They honored the land grant given by Spain to the American, Moses Austin, and they later issued grants to other colonizers. Hundreds of families settled in Texas.

The Austin Colony

Moses Austin applied for a land grant from Spain in 1819 to bring three hundred families to Texas. He promised to settle them in southeast Texas. Austin's request was granted, but he died of pneumonia on June 10, 1821, leaving the work to his son, Stephen F. Austin.

Austin's first settlers entered Texas in December 1821, after Mexico became an independent nation. They settled near present-day Columbus, on the Colorado River, and near Washington-on-the-Brazos. When Austin was later informed that the Mexican government would not recognize the grant issued by the former Spanish colonial government, he traveled to Mexico City to meet with officials. After two years of negotiations, he finally won approval of the grant.

Under the new agreement, each married colonist received a maximum of 4,428 acres of land for ranching and 177 acres for farming. Single colonists received a third of that amount. Austin received 100,000 acres and became leader of the colony.

Austin was granted the right to form a militia to defend the colony. Colonists were not required to pay taxes for six years, but they were required to become Mexican citizens and to convert to Roman Catholicism. Few colonists became Catholic, but Mexico chose not to strictly enforce this regulation. Austin negotiated three other contracts with Mexico, bringing an additional nine hundred families. They settled east of present-day Austin, in Bastrop County, and eastward toward the Gulf Coast.

Life in the Colony

Austin's colony, headquartered on the Brazos River at San Felipe de Austin, fared pretty well. His colonists cleared fields, planted crops, and built log homes, a gristmill, and a cotton gin. They established several stores and started a newspaper. Their crops, mostly cotton and sugarcane, were successful, but money was scarce. Animal pelts became the primary form of barter for coffee, tobacco, and other goods brought in by traders.

Texas colonial families typically lived in log cabins consisting of two rooms separated by a covered breezeway, or "dog run." Heat was provided by rock fireplaces

Rising Conflict

Stephen Austin drew this map of Texas after he and his colonists settled there.

or, where suitable stone was unavailable, by stick-and-mud chimneys. Most cabins had dirt floors, homemade furniture, and no windows.

Life was hard on the frontier, but as more settlers arrived, roads were built, ferries were installed at major river crossings, and towns were founded. The area prospered.

Other Land Developers

Mexico was encouraged by Austin's success and granted colonization permits to Green DeWitt, Martin De León, and others. DeWitt established his colony west of Austin's,

Texas

More Americans than Mexicans lived in Texas by 1830.

near present-day Gonzales, and De León's lay southeast of DeWitt's, near present-day Victoria. Mexico also adopted a democratic constitution in 1824, declaring Texas to be part of Coahuila y Tejas, a state whose capital was Saltillo.

From 1827 to 1830 the population of Austin's colonies expanded to over four thousand, and other colonies also grew. Many colonists came to Nacogdoches, La Bahía, and San Antonio, but others settled where no organized colonies existed, such as north of Galveston Bay, at Liberty. Anglo-Americans soon outnumbered Mexicans in the region.

Rising Conflict

Mexico's Change of Government Leads to a Change of Heart

In 1830 the Mexican government became a dictatorship. This new government viewed the flood of Americans onto its soil as a threat. On April 6, 1830, it tightened its control. Mexico passed a law stopping further American immigration and canceled many contracts with colonizers. The government also sent troops into the area to enforce the new laws.

Texas colonists, including many of Mexican descent, considered these new restrictions unfair and undemocratic. Some colonists took action to protest the April 6 law, and several small battles occurred. These colonists also resented the government's change from democracy to dictatorship, and they were not alone. Rebels from other parts of Mexico overthrew the **dictator**. Rebel leader Antonio López de Santa Anna became Mexico's president in 1833. Texans were happy to see Santa Anna take office. They believed he shared their support of democracy.

Citizens of Texas were surprised and shocked when

Santa Anna declared himself dictator after he became president of Mexico.

Texas settlers did not wish to live under a dictatorship.

Santa Anna later named himself dictator. Most colonists wanted to remain loyal to Mexico's 1824 constitution, but Santa Anna's actions spurred some to call for more. Anglo settlers in Texas, because of their democratic heritage, could not tolerate living under a dictatorship, and Santa Anna's government could not tolerate any resistance among its citizens. Conflict was inevitable.

Chapter Four

War, Republic, and Statehood

Texans attempted to resolve their disagreements with Santa Anna, but had little success. Instead, his government imposed stricter controls, forcing Texans to look for other solutions. What began as a movement in support of a democratic Mexico turned instead into a war for independence, culminating in the famous siege of the Alamo and the Battle of San Jacinto.

Between 1830, when immigration was halted, and 1835, when Santa Anna declared himself dictator of Mexico, two factions developed in Texas. The War Party wanted to break away from Mexico and either form an independent nation or seek statehood in the United States. Members of the Peace Party wanted to try to work things out with Mexico and remain Mexican citizens. For most of those five years, the Peace Party dominated.

Texas citizens felt they needed to voice their opinions about Mexico City's policies, so they held public meetings, one in 1832 and another in 1833. Meetings such as these had been common in the United States, whenever a serious social or political problem arose. Mexican officials, however, became suspicious. They called the meetings "illegal" and suspected Texans had something more in mind.

The Conventions of 1832 and 1833

In October 1832 fifty-eight colonists met in San Felipe to discuss their situation. They chose Stephen F. Austin to lead the meeting. In five days, they drafted petitions to the Mexican government asking that the April 6 immigration law be repealed. They proclaimed loyalty to the Republic of Mexico, and they asked that Texas be declared a separate Mexican state. Because of Mexico's attitude about the meeting, the petitions were never considered.

One year later a second convention again asked for Mexican statehood. Delegates, including William H. Wharton and Sam Houston, wrote a sample state constitution. This time, the convention sent Austin to Mexico City.

When Austin arrived in the capital city, he met with President Santa Anna. Their talks seemed productive, but on his return trip to San Antonio, Austin was arrested. Mexican officials had discovered a letter he had written that was critical of Santa Anna's government. Austin's action was termed treason, and he was imprisoned without a trial.

During the eighteen months Austin was locked in prison, several drastic changes took place in Mexico. Santa

War, Republic, and Statehood

Anna declared the 1824 constitution void, dismissed the Mexican legislature, and declared himself dictator. Austin was released in July 1835. Back in Texas, he found the colonists more upset than ever with Mexico's actions.

Texas Moves Closer to War

When Austin returned he urged Texans to hold another convention to decide what to do. He had long supported peace and cooperation with Mexico, but he surprised many by declaring that war with Santa Anna was unavoidable. He felt Texas would have to fight as a loyal member of the republic, defending the Mexican constitution of 1824.

Considering the mood of most Texas colonists, and the hostile actions of Santa Anna, it was only a matter of

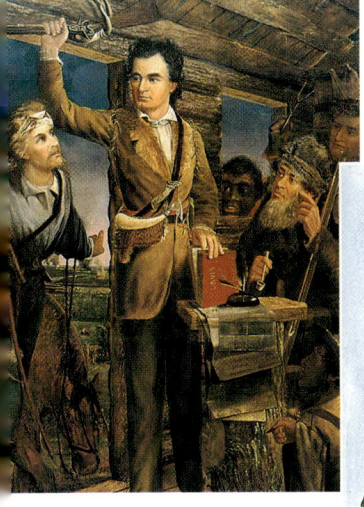

Santa Anna (in the lead below) had Stephen Austin (left) arrested and jailed for treason.

time before a spark would set off the conflict. Such a spark occurred soon. Mexican military leaders in San Antonio remembered that colonists in Gonzales, located sixty miles east of San Antonio, possessed a six-pound cannon. They feared it might be used against Mexican troops.

The Battle of Gonzalez Starts the Texas Revolution

On October 2, 1835, Mexican soldiers tried to take the cannon, but the colonists refused to give it up. Under a banner reading "Come and Take It," they fired on the Mexican troops. One Mexican soldier was killed, and the Mexican force retreated. This brief battle, known as the Battle of Gonzales, started the Texas revolution.

One week later, on October 9, a second **skirmish** took place in Goliad. Mexican troops, under Santa Anna's brother-in-law, General Martín Perfecto de Cós, had been sent to gain control of Texas. Hearing about their approach, Texas volunteers surprised a small portion of de Cós's army and defeated it. The capture of Goliad gave Texas forces a large supply of gunpowder and other badly needed military supplies.

The main body of de Cós's army entered San Antonio and decided to fortify Mission San Antonio de Valero—the Alamo—and defend Mexico's territory from there. The Volunteer Army of Texas, under Stephen F. Austin, marched from Gonzales to San Antonio, arriving there on October 26. Texans laid siege, holding de Cós and his men prisoner in their own stronghold. After two months, de Cós surrendered and

War, Republic, and Statehood

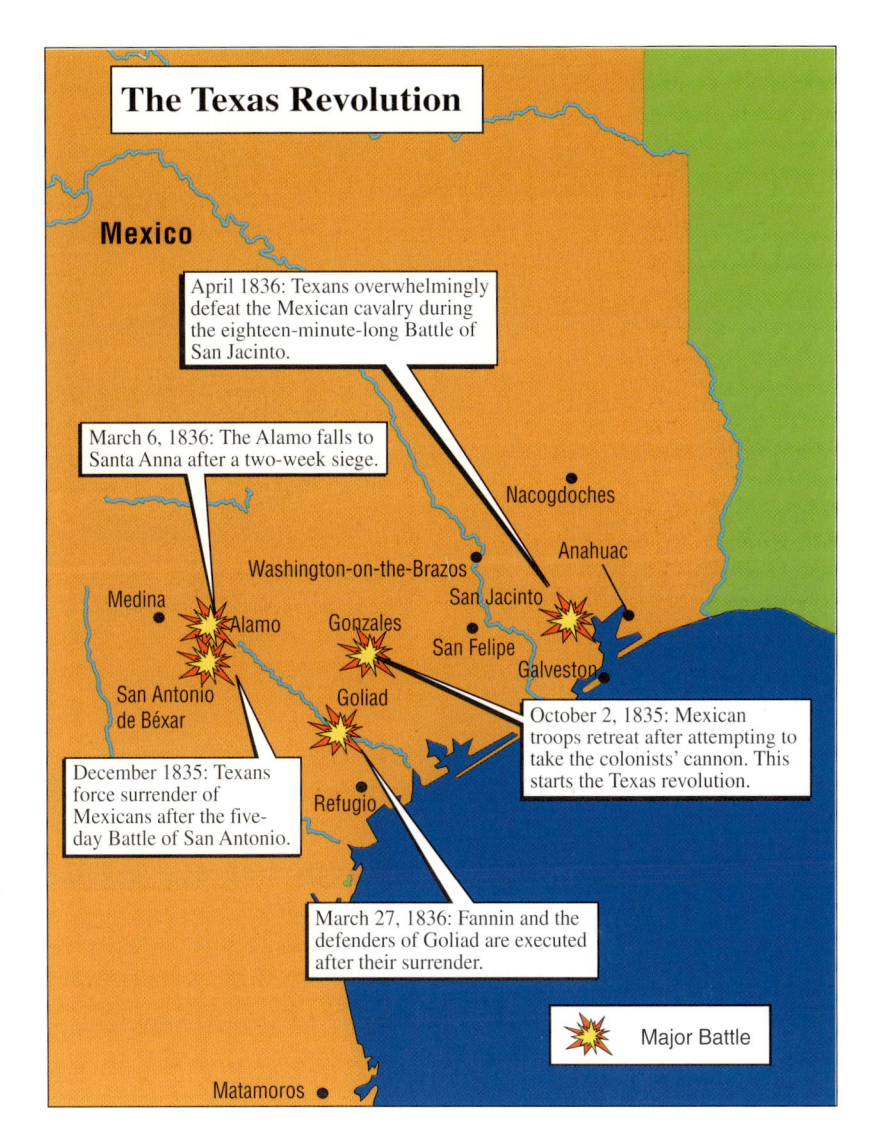

The Texas Revolution

Mexico

April 1836: Texans overwhelmingly defeat the Mexican cavalry during the eighteen-minute-long Battle of San Jacinto.

March 6, 1836: The Alamo falls to Santa Anna after a two-week siege.

Medina • | Alamo | Gonzales | Nacogdoches • | Anahuac
San Antonio de Béxar | Washington-on-the-Brazos | San Jacinto | Galveston
Goliad | San Felipe
Refugio

December 1835: Texans force surrender of Mexicans after the five-day Battle of San Antonio.

October 2, 1835: Mexican troops retreat after attempting to take the colonists' cannon. This starts the Texas revolution.

March 27, 1836: Fannin and the defenders of Goliad are executed after their surrender.

★ Major Battle

Matamoros •

was forced to leave Texas. Texas forces took control of the Alamo.

The Consultation and Santa Anna's Entry into Texas

During the siege of San Antonio, delegates from across Texas held a meeting at San Felipe on November 3, 1835.

31

Texas

Sam Houston was elected commander in chief of the Texas army.

The General Consultation, as the meeting was called, elected Branch T. Archer president of the convention and Sam Houston commander in chief of the Texas army. Delegates decided against a proposal to declare complete independence from Mexico. Instead, they issued another statement in support of Mexico's 1824 constitution. In short, Texans felt they were fighting injustice to protect their rights as citizens of Mexico.

General Santa Anna saw his conflict with the citizens of Texas differently. To him, the Texans were rebels fighting against the legal power of his government. On February 12, 1836, he marched across the Rio Grande into Texas with an army of five thousand, vowing to put down this rebellion and to drive all Anglo-Americans out of Texas.

The Battle of the Alamo

Santa Anna's force arrived in San Antonio on February 23, 1836. Colonel William Barrett Travis, James Bowie, David Crockett, and the volunteers in San Antonio withdrew inside the walls of the Alamo and prepared for battle. The next morning, Santa Anna demanded

War, Republic, and Statehood

the surrender of the 150 men defending the mission. Travis answered with a single cannon shot, and the siege of the Alamo began. For thirteen days Santa Anna's troops bombarded and stormed the fortified mission.

On the evening of the first full day of battle, Travis sent out messages for aid: one to Colonel James W. Fannin at Goliad, one to Texas delegates participating in a second convention, this time in Washington-on-the-Brazos, and a third to the town of Gonzales. Colonel Fannin hesitated to commit his 400 men until it was too late, but 32 volunteers came from Gonzales on March 1 and slipped through enemy lines to enter the Alamo. This increased Travis's forces to 182 men against Santa Anna's 5,000. Desperately hoping other reinforcements

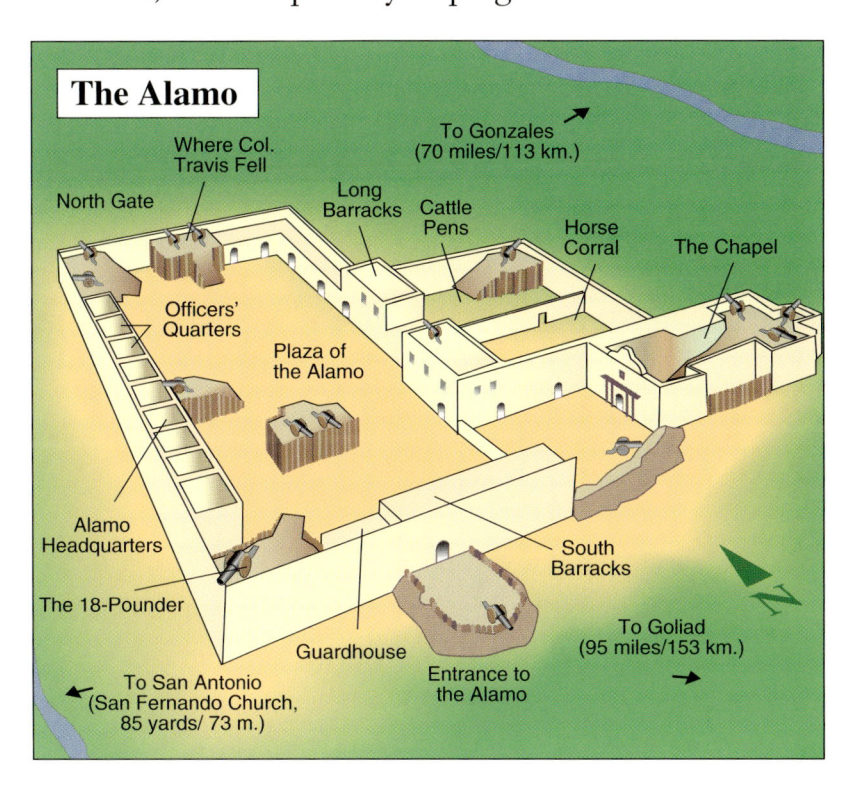

The Alamo

- Where Col. Travis Fell
- To Gonzales (70 miles/113 km.)
- North Gate
- Long Barracks
- Cattle Pens
- Horse Corral
- The Chapel
- Officers' Quarters
- Plaza of the Alamo
- Alamo Headquarters
- South Barracks
- The 18-Pounder
- To Goliad (95 miles/153 km.)
- Guardhouse
- Entrance to the Alamo
- To San Antonio (San Fernando Church, 85 yards/ 73 m.)

Santa Anna and his troops attacked the Alamo for thirteen days.

would arrive, the volunteer army tried to hold on, but the Mexican force was too large.

At 5:00 A.M. on March 6, Santa Anna's bugles sounded the final charge. When the battle ended two hours later, every person who had fought defending the Alamo had been killed. On Santa Anna's orders, the bodies were stacked and burned.

Independence!

The defenders of the Alamo died without hearing about the Texas declaration of independence, adopted in the meeting at Washington-on-the-Brazos on March 2. When they received Travis's call for help, delegates at the meeting made the difficult decision to stay and continue their work.

War, Republic, and Statehood

They felt they could better serve their cause by writing a constitution and establishing a more stable government.

"Remember the Alamo!" became a battle cry for Texas soldiers when they again fought Santa Anna's army at San Jacinto, near present-day Houston. There, on the evening of April 21, 1836, Sam Houston's forces surprised the Mexican army, defeated it, and captured Santa Anna. His surrender led to the Treaty of Velasco, signed on May 14 between Texas and Mexico, ending the Texas revolution. What began as a disagreement over the rights of Mexican citizens led to the birth of a new nation—the Republic of Texas.

The Republic of Texas

After signing the Treaty of Velasco, the Republic of Texas faced new obstacles. It was deeply in debt, having

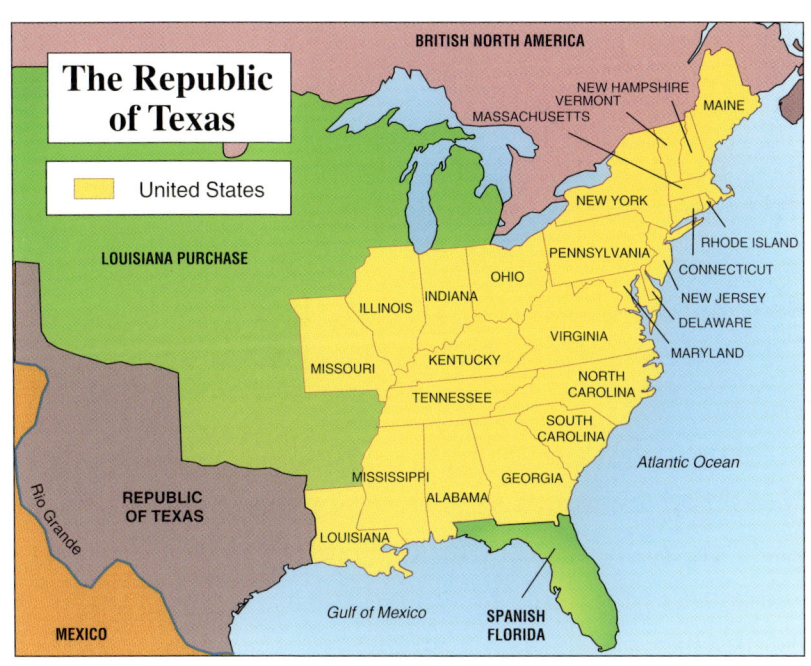

San Antonio stands tall today because of those who fought for Texas's independence.

borrowed over $1 million to finance its war. Republic officials also feared Mexico would invade again, trying to regain the area. Because of this fear, Texas also needed protection from allies. It also needed a permanent government.

At the Washington-on-the-Brazos convention, delegates had chosen a temporary government to govern until elections could be scheduled. David G. Burnet was chosen as president. He called for a general election in September to establish a permanent government, ratify a

War, Republic, and Statehood

constitution, and elect public officials. He also wanted to learn how Texans felt about becoming a U.S. state.

Sam Houston became the republic's first elected president in 1836. He favored seeking statehood, but his successor, Mirabeau B. Lamar, did not. Between 1838 and 1844, Texas applied for statehood several times.

The Struggle for Annexation

From the time Texas first asked to become a U.S. state in 1838, the U.S. Congress had denied its request. Abolitionists, those opposed to slavery, did not want Texas annexed because it allowed slavery. John Quincy Adams, a former U.S. president, led the opposition in Congress, and Secretary of State Daniel Webster, also opposed to slavery, agreed.

By 1844 the opposition had decreased. The United States, under President John Tyler, asked Texas to repeat the request. After a year of debate, Congress passed a joint resolution calling for the **annexation** of Texas. On March 3, 1845, President Tyler signed it into law.

Under the annexation, Texas kept its public lands but signed over military installations to the United States. Texas had to pay its own debts, but it had the option of dividing into as many as five new states. The United States also agreed to negotiate the Rio Grande as Texas's official boundary with Mexico. Texas had to submit a state constitution for approval by the U.S. Congress by January 1846.

The state legislature completed the constitution in 1845, and Congress approved Texas's entry into the

Union. U.S. president James K. Polk signed the legislation on December 29, 1845, and Texas became the twenty-eighth state of the United States, and the largest, with almost as much land area as the original thirteen U.S. colonies combined.

Throughout its history, Texas has always seemed larger than life. Its vast size has inspired awe in those who have visited, and pride in those who have chosen to stay. Its size has also allowed plenty of room for rugged individualism. Texas is the story of these individuals—Indians hunting buffalo on the plains, Spanish and French explorers seeking wealth and fame along the Gulf Coast, colonists struggling to carve out a new life on the frontier, and soldiers fighting for a just cause. Whoever they were, struggle and challenge have always been their companions on their trek through Texas.

Facts About Texas

State capital: Austin
State nickname: Lone Star State
State motto: Friendship
State flower: bluebonnet
State bird: mockingbird
State tree: pecan
State fish: Guadalupe bass
State insect: monarch butterfly
State mammals: armadillo—small mammal
longhorn—large mammal
Mexican free-tailed bat—
flying mammal
State reptile: Texas horned lizard
State song: "Texas, Our Texas"
1998 Population: 19, 760,000
Population density: 74.2 per square mile (1997)
Largest cities: Houston   1,841,064
San Antonio   1,123,626
Dallas   1,085,614
Number of counties: 254
Total area: 267,277 square miles
Highest point: Guadalupe Peak (8,749 ft.)
Lowest point: Gulf of Mexico (sea level)
Gross state product: $551.8 billion (1996)

Texas

Per capita income: $24,957 (1998)

Principal manufactured products: chemicals and allied products, petroleum and coal products, food and kindred products, transportation equipment

Principal agricultural products: cattle, cotton, dairy products, nursery and greenhouse products

Principal minerals: petroleum, natural gas, natural gas liquids

Glossary

Ahahayo: "Father Above"—the supreme deity or god of the Caddo

annexation: Being added to a group. Texas was annexed as the twenty-eighth state in the United States.

breechclout: a piece of leather or cloth worn around the waist

confederation: an alliance or union between groups of people

dictator: someone who has complete control of a country, often ruling it unjustly

hunter-gatherers: Native Americans who lived by hunting animals and gathering edible plants

maize: a type of corn

nomads: people who move from place to place in search of food, water, and shelter.

pinole: roots, nuts, and dried fruit ground into flour for making bread

skirmish: a short battle

wickiup: a crude round shelter made from branches and covered with grass

For Further Exploration

Books

Judy Alter, *Sam Houston: A Leader for Texas.* Danbury, CT: Childrens Press, 1998. A biography of Sam Houston, who served as a congressman and governor of Tennessee before becoming associated with Texas.

Jean Flynn and Buddy Mullin, *Stephen F. Austin: The Father of Texas.* Austin, TX: Eakin, 1993. A biography of the Texas pioneer and leader in the Texas revolution of 1835 and 1836.

Ann Graham Gaines, *Jim Bowie: Hero of the Alamo.* Springfield, NJ: Enslow, 2000. This book traces the life of the frontier settler and Texas defender who died in the attack on the Alamo. It includes information on his early days and his effect on the American frontier culture.

Ann Heinrichs, *Texas.* Danbury, CT: Childrens Press, 1999. A comprehensive look at Texas: history, geography, cities and towns, government, economics, art, sports, famous Texans, statistics, demographics, state symbols, and more.

Mary Deborah Petite, *1836 Facts About the Alamo and the Texas War for Independence.* El Dorado Hills, CA: Savas, 1999. This book offers little-known facts about the Alamo and Texas's fight for independence from Mexico.

George E. Sullivan, *Alamo!* New York: Scholastic, 1997. A historical account of the 1836 battle for indepen-

For Further Exploration

dence from Mexico, including the events that led up to it, the people involved, and the aftermath.

Kathleen Thompson, *Texas*. Austin, TX: Raintree Steck-Vaughn, 1996. Discusses the history, economy, culture, and future of Texas. Also includes a state chronology, pertinent statistics, and maps.

Lon Tinkle, *Thirteen Days to Glory: The Siege of the Alamo*. College Station: Texas A&M University Press, 1996. An excellent narrative about the battle fought at the Alamo.

Websites

The State of Texas: www.state.tx.us

Texas tourism: www.traveltex.com

Texas history: www.tsha.utexas.edu/handbook/online

Index

Adams, John Quincy, 37
Ahahayo (Caddo god), 8
Alabama (tribe), 21
Alamo, 17, 30–31
　Battle of, 32–34
Archer, Branch T., 32
Austin, Moses, 21
Austin, Stephen F.,
　21–22, 28–29, 30

Bowie, James, 32–34
buffalo, 8
Burnet, David G., 36

Cabeza de Vaca, Álvar
　Núñez, 13–15
Caddo, 5, 6–8, 16
cannibalism, 9, 11
Cherokee, 21
climate, 5
clothing, 7
Coahuiltecan, 5–6
colonists
　in Austin colony, 21–23
　early, 20–31
　ideas of, 19–20, 26–27
　increase in number of,
　23–24
　from Spain, 16
Comanche, 17–18
constitutions, 35, 37
conventions, 28, 33, 36
Coronado, Francisco
　Vásquez, 15
Coushatta, 21
Crockett, David, 32–34

de Cós, Martín Perfecto,
　30
Delaware, 21
de Soto, Hernando, 15
DeWitt, Green, 23–24

explorers
　Cabeza de Vaca, 13–15
　Coronado, 15
　de Soto, 15
　La Salle, 16

Fannin, James W., 33
food
　of Caddo, 7
　of Karankawa, 11
　of Tonkawa, 8

44

Index

France, 16

Galveston Island, 13
General Consultation, 32
Goliad, Battle of, 30
Gonzales, Battle of, 30
government, 7

homes
  of Caddo, 6
  of colonists, 22–23
  of Karankawa, 10
  of Tonkawa, 8
Houston, Sam, 28, 32, 35, 37
hunter-gatherers, 8, 9

Indians
  cultures of, 5–6
  first arrival of, 4
  see also names of tribes
Island of Doom, 14

Karankawa, 5–6, 9–11, 14
Kickapoo, 21
Kiowa, 5

Lamar, Mirabeau B., 37
land grants, 21–24

La Salle, René-Robert Cavelier, Sieur de, 16
León, Alonso de, 16
León, Martin De, 23, 24
Lipan Apache, 5
location, 4
maize, 7
Malhado, 14
Massanet, Damián, 16
Mexico
  border of, 37
  government of, 20, 25, 27–29
  independence of, 18
  land grants and, 21–24
  missions, 16–17
  motto, 4
  mounds, 8

name, 4
nomads, 4, 8, 9

Peace Party, 27
People of the Wolf, 8
Polk, James K., 38
population, 4, 24

religion
  of Caddo, 8
  of Karankawa, 11

of Tonkawa, 9
Republic of Texas, 35–37
Roman Catholicism, 16, 22

Sacred Fire, 8
San Antonio de Valero. *See* Alamo
San Francisco de los Tejas, 16
San Jacinto, Battle of, 35
Santa Anna, Antonio López de, 25–29, 32–34, 35
Seven Cities of Gold, 15
Shawnee, 21
size, 4
slavery, 37
Spain
  colonists from, 16
  Comanche and, 18
  explorers from, 13–16
statehood
  in Mexico, 28
  in United States, 37–38

Tejano, 20
Texas Revolution, 30–34
Tonkawa, 5, 8–9
Travis, William Barrett, 32–34
Tyler, John, 37

Velasco, Treaty of, 35
villages, 6
Volunteer Army of Texas, 30

War Party, 27
Webster, Daniel, 37
Wharton, William H., 28
Wichitas, 5
wickiups, 8
wigwams, 10
women, 7

Picture Credits

Cover: Hulton/Archive by Getty Images
© Bettmann/CORBIS, 15, 32
© D. Donne Bryant/Art Resource, 17
© Christie's Images/CORBIS, 9
© CORBIS, 23
DigitalVision, 34
© Philip Gould/CORBIS, 7
© Hulton/Archive by Getty Images, 13, 20, 25, 26
© Hulton-Deutsch/CORBIS, 10
Chris Jouan, 5, 6, 31, 33, 35
© Danny Lehman/CORBIS, 19
© North Wind Pictures, 14, 24, 29
Smithsonian American Art Museum, Washington D.C./Art Resource, 18
© Lee Snider/CORBIS, 36
State Preservation Board, Austin, Texas, 29

About the Authors

Charles and Linda George have written more than thirty nonfiction books for children and teens. They were both teachers in Texas public schools before retiring to write full time. Charles taught secondary history and Spanish, and Linda taught in the elementary grades. They live in the mountains of New Mexico, near the village of Cloudcroft.